ZOOM IN ON
FIREFLIES

Melissa Stewart

ZOOM
In on
Insects!

W9-BNA-757

Enslow Elementary

CONTENTS

WORDS TO KNOW

antennae (an TEN ee)— Two long, thin body parts on the head of insects and some other animals. Antennae help animals sense the world around them.

lantern (LAN tern)—The part of a firefly's body that gives off light. It is in the abdomen.

larva (LAHR vuh)—The second part in the life cycle of some insects. A larva changes into a pupa.

nectar (NEK tuhr)—A sugary liquid that many flowers make. Some fireflies drink it.

pupa (PYOO puh)—The third part in the life cycle of some insects. A pupa changes into an adult.

FIREFLY HOMES

ZOOM BUBBLE

Fireflies live in many parts of the world. In some places, people call them lightning bugs.

These insects like warm, damp places away from lights. You can find them near ponds and streams. Look for them in fields and backyards, too.

PARTS OF A FIREFLY

antenna

head

thorax

wing

eye

leg

abdomen

lantern

FIREFLY BODY

ZOOM BUBBLE

A firefly is not a fly. It belongs to a group of insects called beetles. It has six legs. And its body has three parts. They are the head, the thorax, and the abdomen.

FIREFLY FLASH

Fireflies are famous for their flash. Why do they glow? They rest during the day and come out at night. They use the lantern on their back end to find mates in the dark.

FIREFLY LEGS

A firefly has six legs. They are attached to the middle of its body.

Female fireflies spend most of their time on the ground. They use their legs to walk from place to place. Males spend much more time flying.

FIREFLY WINGS

ZOOM BUBBLE

Most fireflies have two sets of wings. The front wings protect the back wings. When a firefly is ready to fly, it lifts the front wings. Then it spreads the back wings and takes off. The back wings flap through the air.

This female firefly is flashing its lantern in the grass.

FIREFLY EYES

ZOOM BUBBLE

A firefly has two huge eyes. They can see right and left, up and down— all at the same time.

A male firefly needs to see well. He uses his eyes to spot flashing females in the grass.

FIREFLY ANTENNAE

ZOOM BUBBLE

A firefly has two long antennae on its head. Some are straight. Others are feathery. But they all do the same things. They can feel and hear and smell.

FIREFLY FOOD

ZOOM BUBBLE

Most adult fireflies do not eat at all. They live on fat stored in their bodies.

Some fireflies sip sweet, sugary nectar from plants. A few eat other kinds of insects.

FIREFLY GLOWWORMS

When a firefly comes out of its egg, it looks like a worm. It gives off a soft light.

The glowworm hunts slugs, worms, and snails. It eats and grows for up to two years. Then it becomes a **pupa**.

LIFE CYCLE

A firefly begins life inside an EGG.

A firefly LARVA is called a glowworm.

ADULT fireflies live just a few days. Most of them don't eat at all.

On the outside, a PUPA stays still. But its body is changing inside.

LEARN MORE

BOOKS

Ashley, Susan. *Incredible Fireflies.* Milwaukee: Gareth Stevens, 2011.

Hudak, Heather C., ed. *Fireflies.* New York: Weigl Publishers, 2009.

Miller, Connie Colwell. *Fireflies.* Mankato, Minn.: Capstone Press, 2005.

Rau, Dana Meachen. *Flash, Firefly, Flash!* New York: Marshall Cavendish Benchmark, 2008.

WEB SITES

National Geographic. *Firefly.*
<http://animals.nationalgeographic.com/animals/bugs/firefly>

Ready, Set, Glow! *Activity Sheets.*
<http://readysetglow.org/activitysheets/index.html>

INDEX

Enslow Elementary, an imprint of Enslow Publishers, Inc.
Enslow Elementary® is a registered trademark of Enslow
Publishers, Inc.

Copyright © 2014 by Melissa Stewart

Library of Congress Cataloging-in-Publication Data

Stewart, Melissa.
Zoom in on fireflies / Melissa Stewart.
p. cm. — (Zoom in on insects!)
Summary: "Provides information for readers about a
firefly's home, food, and body"—Provided by publisher.
Includes index.
ISBN 978-0-7660-4213-1
1. Fireflies—Juvenile literature. I. Title. II. Series: Stewart,
Melissa. Zoom in on insects.
QL596.L28S74 2014
595.7644—dc23

2012040389

Paperback ISBN: 978-1-4644-0369-9
EPUB ISBN: 978-1-4645-1204-9
Single-User PDF ISBN: 978-1-4646-1204-6
Multi-User PDF ISBN: 978-0-7660-5836-1

Printed in the United States of America

10 9 8 7 6 5 4 3 2 1

Series Literacy Consultant:
Allan A. De Fina, PhD
Past President of the New Jersey Reading Association
Chairperson, Department of Literacy Education
New Jersey City University
Jersey City, New Jersey

Science Consultant:
Helen Hess, PhD
Professor of Biology
College of the Atlantic
Bar Harbor, Maine

To Our Readers: We have done our best to make sure all Internet
Addresses in this book were active and appropriate when we went
to press. However, the author and the publisher have no control
over and assume no liability for the material available on those
Internet sites or on other Web sites they may link to. Any
comments or suggestions can be sent by e-mail to comments@
enslow.com or to the address on the back cover.

Enslow Publishers, Inc., is committed to printing our books
on recycled paper. The paper in every book contains 10% to 30%
post-consumer waste (PCW). The cover board on the outside of
each book contains 100% PCW. Our goal is to do our part to help
young people and the environment too!

Photo Credits: David Cappaert, Michigan State University,
Bugwood.org, pp. 10, 11; © James E. Lloyd/Animals Animals,
p. 18; Kazuo Unno/Nature Production/Minden Pictures, p. 22
(bottom right); Dr. Paul Zahl/Science Source/Getty Images, p. 9;
Ivan Kuzmin/Alamy Stock Photo. p. 12; Paul A. Zahl/National
Geographic/Getty Images, p. 15; © Dwight Kuhn, pp. 1, 4, 6, 16,
19, 20, 22 (top left, top right); WildPictures/Alamy Stock Photo, p.
13; Yukihiro Fukuda/Nature Picture Library/Getty Images, p. 8;
Satoshi Kuribayashi/Nature Production/Minden Pictures, pp.
21, 22 (bottom left); Shane Cummins/Photos.com, p. 17;
Shutterstock.com, p. 2, 3, 7; Richard Packwood/Getty Images,
p. 14; Tyler Fox/Photos.com, p. 5.
Cover Photo: © Dwight Kuhn

Enslow Elementary
an imprint of
Enslow Publishers, Inc.
40 Industrial Road
Box 398
Berkeley Heights, NJ 07922
USA
http://www.enslow.com